MY FATHER'S WORLD

MASTERPIECES AND MEMORIES OF THE GREAT OUTDOORS

THOMAS KINKADE

THOMAS KINKADE *Painter of Light*™

Publishers Since 1798

THOMAS NELSON PUBLISHERS®
Nashville

My Father's World

THOMAS NELSON PUBLISHERS®
Nashville

Published in Nashville, Tennessee, by Thomas Nelson, Inc.

Scripture quotations are from the NEW KING JAMES VERSION of the Bible. Copyright © 1979, 1980, 1982, Thomas Nelson, Inc., Publishers.

Design and production by: Quebecor World Digital Services, Chicago

Presented to:

_____

On this _15_ day

of _June_

By _Sarah_

_____

With this special message:

I love you

_____

_____

_____

_____

_____

Dark is the night, and fitful and drearily

Rushes the wind, like the waves of the sea!

Little care I, as here I sit cheerily,

Wife at my side and baby on my knee:

King, king, crown me king:

Home is the kingdom and love is the king!

– WILLIAM RANKIN DWYER

Special memories of our times together…

One of my happiest memories is of the day I got married and you walked me down the isle. It ment the world to me that you were there despite everything + everyone that was there. I love you.

To get his goodnight kiss he stood
Beside my chair one night
And raised an eager face to me,
A face with love alight.

And as I gathered in my arms
The son God gave to me,
I thanked the lad for being good,
And hoped he'd always be.

His little arms crept 'round my neck,
And then I heard him say
Four simple words I can't forget—
Four words that made me pray.

They turned a mirror on my soul,
on secrets no one knew,
They startled me, I hear them yet:
He said, "I'll be like you."

— HERBERT PARKER

8

Watch your thoughts; they become your words.

Watch your words; they become your actions.

Watch your actions; they become your habits.

Watch your habits; they become your character.

Watch your character; it becomes your destiny.

— Frank Outlaw

One of the rarest things a man can do is to do
the best he can.

— Henry Wheeler Shaw

A little child, a limber elf,

Singing, dancing to itself…

Makes such a vision to the sight

As fills a father's eyes with light.

– SAMUEL TAYLOR COLERIDGE

Many an excellent man is tempted to
forget that the best offering he can
make to his children is himself.

– HENRY NEUMAN

Thomas Kinkade

And yet . . . there were those times Dad would take us with him on his footloose adventures. And what unforgettable times those were!

– THOMAS KINKADE

Each evening that I am at home I oversee their bedtime preparations—brushing teeth, administering baths, putting on pajamas, saying prayers, and hauling four to six glasses of water to each little procrastinator.

– JAMES DOBSON

A man never knows how to be a son until he becomes a father…. By the time a man realizes that maybe his father was right, he usually has a son who thinks he is wrong.

– AUTHOR UNKNOWN

Train up a child in the way he should go and when he is old he will not depart from it.

– PROVERBS 22:6

16

To the child, the father is God's representative; this makes the father's task sacred and serious. We fathers are to deal with our children as God deals with us.

– JOHN DRESCHER

When the Father exercises a leadership role in family worship, the other roles or expectations seem to fall into place.

– BILL AND PAT BOUCHILLON

A personal note…

I love you very much.
I know there have been
alot of hard times in
the past. I know you
will always be my
dad and you will
always be there for
me and my family

A careful man I want to be,

A little fellow follows me;

I do not dare go astray,

For fear he'll go the self-same way.

I cannot once escape his eyes;

Whatever he sees me do he tries;

Like me he says he wants to be—

That little chap who follows me.

He thinks that I am big and fine,

He believes in every word of mine;

The base in me he does not see—

This little chap who follows me.

I must remember as I go

Through summer sun and winter snow,

I'm building for the years to be—

That little chap who follows me.

Lord, if I his guide must be,

O let the little children see

A teacher leaning hard on Thee.

— MARVIN BAARMAN

Romance fails us and so do friendships,
but the relationship of parent and child,
less noisy than all others, remains indelible
and indestructible, the strongest
relationship on earth.

– THEODOR REIK

A happy childhood is one of the best gifts
that parents have in their power to bestow.

– R. CHOLMONDELEY

We need love's tender lessons taught

As only weakness can;

God hath His small interpreter;

The child must teach the man.

– John Greenleaf Whittier

Children a poor men's riches.

– Thomas Fuller

When I was a boy of fourteen, my father
was so ignorant I could hardly stand to
have the old man around. But, when I got
to be twenty-one, I was astonished at how
much he had learned in seven years.

– MARK TWAIN

You don't raise heroes you raise sons.
If you treat them like sons, they'll be
heroes, even if it's just in your eyes.

– WALTER SCHIRRA, SR.

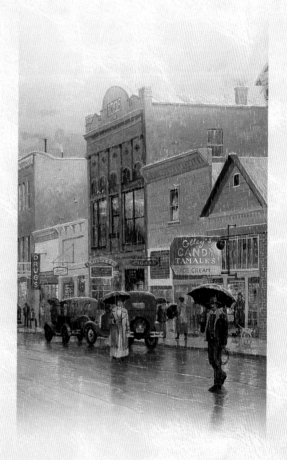

To be a good parent, you have to put
yourself second, to recognize that the child
has feelings and needs separate from yours,
and fulfill those needs without expecting
anything in return.

– HOWARD KOOGAN

How can one say no to a child? How can
one be anything but a slave to one's own
flesh and blood?

– HENRY MILLER

Fathers should not get discouraged if their sons reject their advice. It will not be wasted; years later the sons will offer it to their own offspring.

– AUTHOR UNKNOWN

Loving relationships are a family's best protection against the challenges of the world.

– BERNIE WIEBE

One of my happiest memories of you is…

on the day you got married. It was wonderful to stand up there with you on one of your happiest days.

Ten Commandments for Fathers:

1. A father should strive to be a whole person.

2. A father should love his children.

3. A father should love his wife.

4. A father should be creative.

5. A father should raise his children to leave him.

6. A father should spend time with his children.

7. A father should communicate with his children.

8. A father should discipline his children properly.

9. A father should develop a sense of humor.

10. A father should enjoy being a father.

— HENRY JAMES CARGAS

I see, Lord, from hence, that my father's piety cannot be entailed; that is bad news for me. But I see also that actual impiety is not always hereditary; that is good news for my son.

– THOMAS FULLER

A wise son makes a glad father.

– PROVERBS 10:1

He never cares to wander from his own fireside,

He never cares to wander or to roam.

With his baby on his knee,

He's as happy as can be,

For there's no place like home, sweet home.

– FELIX MCGLENNON

The mark of a good parent is that he can have
fun while being one.

– MARCELENE COX

A child enters your home and for the next twenty years makes so much noise that you can hardly stand it. The child departs, leaving the house so silent you think you are going mad.

– John Andrew Holmes

Happy is he that is happy in his children.

– Thomas Fuller

In our dealings with men, however unkind
and hurting they are, we must exercise the
same patience as God exercises with us.
It is the simple truth that such patience is
not the sign of weakness but the sign of
strength; it is not defeatism, but rather
the only way to victory.

– WILLIAM BARCLAY

What shall you give to one small boy?

A glamorous game, a tinseled toy,

A fancy knife, a puzzle pack,

A train that runs on a curving track,

A picture book, a real live pet?

No! There's plenty of time for such things yet.

Give him a day for his very own.

Just one small boy and his dad alone.

A walk in the woods a romp in the park,

A fishing trip from dawn to dark.

Give him the finest gift you can—

The companionship of a grown up man.

Games are outgrown, and toys decay,

But he'll never forget the gift of a day!

    – AUTHOR UNKNOWN

Special memories of our times together…

To show a child what once has delighted you, to find the child's delight added to your own so that there is now a double delight seen in the glow of trust and affection, this is happiness.

– J. B. Piestley

To provide some degree of child training at home requires that both parents and children be there at the same time.

– Dr. Harold Smith

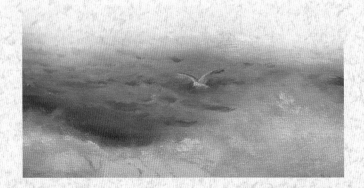

In the effort to give good and comforting
answers to the young questioners whom
we love, we very often arrive at good and
comforting answers for ourselves.

– AUTHOR UNKNOWN

The child you want to raise as an upright
and honorable person requires a lot more
of your time than your money.

– GEORGE VARKY

Don't demand respect as a parent.
Demand civility and insist in honesty.
But respect is something you must earn—
with kids as well as adults.

– WILLIAM ATTWOOD

By profession I am a soldier and take
pride in that fact. But I am prouder,
infinitely prouder, to be a father.

– GENERAL DOUGLAS MCARTHUR

Thomas
Kinkade

If Christ lives in us, controlling our
personalities, we will leave glorious marks
on the lives we touch. Not because of our
character but because of His.

– Eugenia Price

A child is not likely to find a father in God
unless he finds something of God in his father.

– Austin L. Sorensen

We know that the secret of America's
success has been our drive to excel,
a spirit born and nurtured by our families.
With their dreams and hard work, they've
built our nation, made her great, and
kept her good. Everything we've
accomplished began in those bedrock
values parents have sought to impart
throughout our history—values of faith
in God, honesty, caring for others, personal
responsibility, thrift and initiative.

– RONALD REAGAN

I have found the best way to give advice to
your children is to find out what they want
and then advise them to do it.

– HARRY S. TRUMAN

Respect the child. Be not too much his
parent. Trespass not on his solitude.

– RALPH WALDO EMERSON

Doesn't matter who my father was;
it matters who I remember he was.

– ANNE SEXTON

A personal note...

I miss you very much.
now that we are
close after all that time
apart you left again.
I know you are happy
and that makes me
happy.

Father's Day—When a man who is proud
of his family finds his family is proud of him.

– ANONYMOUS

The righteous man walks in his integrity;
his children are blessed after him.

– PROVERBS 20:7

The value of marriage is not that adults
produce children, but that children
produce adults.

– PETER DEVRIES

Man is wise and constantly in quest for more wisdom; but the ultimate wisdom which deals with beginnings, remains locked in a seed.

– HAL BORLAND

Behold what manner of love the Father has bestowed on us, that we should be called children of God!

– 1 JOHN 3:1

Father is God's special representative in the home. As the family's divinely appointed priest and intercessor he is the spiritual leader. He is responsible for the daily intercession for the mother and each individual child. He is also responsible for beginning and maintaining the domestic altar each day, and for adequate Christian education of mother and children.

– GORDON CHILVERS

Nothing is dearer to a father than a daughter.
Sons have spirits of higher pitch, but sons
aren't given to showing affection.

– Euripedes

He who has daughters is always a Shepherd.

– Spanish Proverb

It is not enough for parents to understand
children. They must accord children the
privilege of understanding them.

– Milton R. Saperstein

He that will have his son have a respect for him and his orders, must himself have a great reverence for his son.

– JOHN LOCKE

What a father says to his children is not heard by the world, but it will be heard by posterity.

– JEAN PAUL RICHTER

It is a wise father that knows his own child.

– WILLIAM SHAKESPEARE

If you read history you will find that the
Christians who did the most for the present
world are those who thought the most of the next.

      – C. S. Lewis

There can be hope for a society which acts as
one big family, and not as many separate ones.

      – Anwar El-Sadat

The family that prays together stays together.

      – Author Unknown

These are some things you taught me that
I hope to pass on to my children…

Could I turn back the time machine, I would give double the attention I gave to my children and go to fewer meetings.

– J.D. Eppinga

Every father is the world's best father to his children unless he works hard not to be.

– E. Carl Wilson

It is easier to build boys than to mend men.

– Author unknown

We can never afford to forget that we
teach our children to call God father,
and the only conception of fatherhood
that they can have is the conception
which we give them. Human fatherhood
should be molded and modeled on the
pattern of the fatherhood of God.
It is the tremendous duty of the human
father to be as good a father as God.

– WILLIAM BARCLAY

The night you were born I ceased being my
father's boy and became my son's father.
That night I began a new life.

– HENRY GREGOR FELSON

There are only two lasting bequests we can
hope to give our children. One of these is
roots, the other wings.

– HODDING CARTER

A *Newsweek* article reported that middle class American fathers spend an average of fifteen to twenty minutes per day with their children. In many cases even if the fathers are present physically, they are absent relationally. We need men who will place their families as the number one priority in their lives. Men who will give as much of themselves to their children as they do their work.

– JAMES A. HARNISH

Don't take up a man's time talking about the smartness of your children; he wants to talk to you about the smartness of his own children.

– ED HOWE

Children are unpredictable. You never know what inconsistency they are going to catch you in next.

– FRANKLIN P. JONES

Children's children are the crown of old men,

and the glory of children is their father.

– Proverbs 17:6

Father! To God himself we cannot give a holier name.

– William Wordsworth

If you must hold yourself up to your children, hold

yourself up as an object lesson not as an example.

– George Bernard Shaw

Special memories of our times together…

_____

_____

_____

_____

_____

_____

_____

_____

_____

_____

_____

_____

Parents lend children their experience
and vicarious memory; children endow
their parents with a vicarious immortality.

– GEORGE SANTAYANA

Before I got married I had six theories
about bringing up children. Now I have
six children and no theories.

– JOHN WILMOT

It behooves a father to be blameless if
he expects his son to be.

– HOMER

We have learned from Freud and others about those distortions in character and errors in thought which result from a man's early conflicts with his father. For the most important thing we know about George MacDonald is that his whole life illustrates the opposite process. An almost perfect relationship with his father was the earthly root of all his wisdom. From his own father, he said, he first learned that fatherhood must be at the core of the universe. He was thus prepared in an unusual way to teach that religion in which the relation of the Father and Son is of all relations the most central.

– C. S. LEWIS

Becoming a father is easy enough.
But being one is rough.

– WILHELM BUSCH

I could not point to any need in
childhood as strong as that for a
father's protection.

– SIGMUND FREUD

Blood's thicker than water, and
when one's in trouble, best seek
out a relative's open arms.

– EURIPIDES

Thomas Kinkade

To bring up a child in the way he should go,
travel that way yourself once in a while.

– Josh Billings

Children need models rather than critics.

– Joseph Joubert

The father in praising his son praises himself.

– Chinese Proverb

When the Romanian pastor Richard Wurmbrandt and his wife were thrown into prison by the communists, their nine-year-old son was hauled off to a government school to be indoctrinated in Marxism and atheism. Some years later as a method of psychological torture for his parents, the boy was brought to see them for the purpose of denouncing Christ to their faces. As he studied the marks of suffering on his father's face together with the joy evidenced in his mother's spirit, he suddenly declared, "If Christ means this much to you then I want Him too." Years of intensive brainwashing evaporated with only a touch of Christlike influence.

– AUTHOR UNKNOWN

The most important thing that parents can teach their children is how to get along without them.

— FRANK CLARK

The sooner you treat your son as a man the sooner he will be one.

— JOHN DRYDEN

There is never much trouble in any family where the children hope some day to resemble their parents.

— WILLIAM LYON PHELPS

A personal note…

The most important thing that any father
can do for his children is love their mother.

– THEODORE HESBURGH

If you make children happy now, you will
make them happy twenty years hence by
the memory of it.

– KATE DOUGLAS WIGGIN

Father: Someone we can look up to no
matter how tall we get.

– AUTHOR UNKNOWN

The chances are that you will never be elected president of the country, write the great American novel, make a million dollars, stop pollution, end racial conflict, or save the world. However valid it may be to work at any of these goals, there is another one of higher priority—to be an effective parent.

– LANDRUM B. ROLLING

It is better to bind your children to you
by respect and gentleness than by fear.

– TERENCE

Children's children are the crown of
old men, and the glory of children is
their father.

– PROVERBS 17:6

Force may subdue, but love gains;
he that forgives first wins the laurel.

– WILLIAM PENN

A family is a unit composed not only of
children but of men, women, an
occasional animal, and the common cold.

— OGDEN NASH

If man leaves little children behind him,
it is as if he did not die.

— MOROCCAN PROVERB

The commonest axiom of history is that
every generation revolts against its fathers
and makes friends with its grandfathers.

— LEWIS MUMFORD

It is a wise child that knows its own father, and an unusual one that unreservedly approves of him.

– MARK TWAIN

Happy that man whose children make his happiness in life and not his grief.

– EURIPIDES

What children hear at home soon flies abroad.

– THOMAS FULLER

Happy is the father whose child finds his attempts to amuse it amusing.

– Robert Lynd

Reasoning with a child is fine, if you can reach the child's reason without destroying your own.

– John Mason Brown

I do not love him because he is good, but because he is my little child.

– Rabindranath Tagore

Thank you for your godly example.
I hope to be more like you in these ways.

If they obey and serve Him, they shall spend their days in prosperity, and their years in pleasures.

– Job 36:11

But as many as received Him, to them He gave the right to be called children of God.

– John 1:12

Behold, children are a heritage from the LORD.

– Psalm 127:3

I thank my God upon every remembrance of you.

– Philippians 1:3

Like arrows in the hand of a warrior;

So are the children of one's youth.

Happy is the man whose quiver is full of them;

They shall not be ashamed,

But shall speak with their enemies in the gate.

– Psalm 127:4-5

The glory of young men is their strength, and
the splendor of old men is their gray head.

– Proverbs 21:29

Example is not the main thing in
influencing others—it is the only thing.

— ALBERT SCHWEITZER

The art of praising is the beginning of
the fine art of pleasing.

— GEORGE W. CRANE

This is the duty of a father, to
accustom his son to act rightly of his
own accord than from unnatural fear.

— TERENCE

You don't choose your family.

They are God's gift to you, as you are to them.

– DESMOND TUTU

A happy family is but an earlier heaven.

– SIR JOHN BOWRING

We've had bad luck with our kids—

they've all grown up.

– CHRISTOPHER MORLEY